SPACE FOR MORE …

JSRN – Just Start Right Now With What You Have!!!

Paul Anthony Edwards

ISBN 978-976-95970-0-6

Published in Jamaica by Seven Quotients (7quotients@gmail.com)
Webpage: fb.me/7quotientsspace4more;
Instagram: @7quotientsspace4more
Facebook #space4more #relationships #moneymatters
#generationalabundance #EEHvibration #DivineNatureAttributesDNA
#MyNewMoneyMindset #personalharmometer

WHY READ THIS BOOK

Space for More ... Just Start Right Now with What You Have by Paul Anthony Edwards is a powerful book, or more appropriately, a powerful self-improvement manual in the art and science of developing the 7 aspects of your being and living. Space for More is so very easy to read. It is just like talking with Paul or listening to him present. It conveys all of the essential elements that need to be communicated without undue fluff. It is straight-forward and to the point. His stories with Sharee, Jean-Luke and about multi-dimensional sex are just awesome.

In 2010, Paul introduced me to the Personal Harmometer ® and the 7 aspects of being that he has so effortlessly and elegantly presented in this book. My credit-card-sized Harmometer ® has not left my wallet since. I have used it with great success in enhancing the harmony among my 7 aspects to the point that it (along with training from my spiritual support centre — the Universal Centre of Truth for Better Living) has contributed to my own book, Personal Mastery: Maximize Your Potential Now!

These two books build upon and support each other to deliver extraordinary value to the readers and users. Personal Mastery helps you to create strategic life plans for the 7 dimensions of your being. Paul's Space for More opens up room for you to create and get more of all the good things you need in your new, better, more harmonious life, through a simple but effective measurement tool for ALL-7 dimensions. With Paul's Harmometer® you always have a friend close at hand. Get it. Use it. JSRN – Just Start Right Now with What You Have and create Space for More.

> ---Courtney Lodge, Author,
> Personal Mastery: Maximize Your
> Potential Now!

WHY READ THIS BOOK

This book has relevance for all ages and all stages of life.

ROBYN – University Medical Student (before 25 years old) Kingston - Jamaica. "The tools and systems in this book are just awesome. From I was 13, I was able to develop a vision of what I pictured my life would be like at 25 yo that felt right for me in all 7-areas of life (Personal Harmometer ®). I have been stepping forward into that vision with passion and energy ever since."

DANIELLE – Specialist Math Teacher (25-35 yo) Kingston – Jamaica. "Working with the systems contained within this book helped me to move, just before my 24th birthday, into my own rental two bedroom, two bathroom apartment, paid for by my part-time business (tutoring math) without any need to touch my teachers' salary from my full-time employment. Then 4 years later, in line with the clarity of "Who I am", "What's my purpose" and "Actions to take" I confidently relocated to Singapore to take up a 3-year Math Teaching Contract just before Christmas 2015. It would take a separate book to speak about my husband and I coming together and the influence of the 3-Step Harmony Formula and the Personal Harmometer ®."

WILLIS – Security Guard, Business Farmer (35-45 yo) Christiana – Jamaica. "Mr. Edwards, things have been so good and much easier for me and my family. I have been through a lot in life. With your inspiration, business advice and encouragement, I have put myself in a position where hunger will never be my best friend again. God bless you."

COURTNEY (45-55 yo) see his comments on the previous page

ANTHONY Dad and Grandad (more than 55 yo) Mandeville – Jamaica. "Armed with the tools, system and techniques within this book, I can now more systematically share my experiences and wisdom with the generations behind me, equipping them for life to ultimately do the same from generation to generation."

Table of Contents

USING THIS GUIDE AND WORKBOOK

1. Using this Guide & Workbook

In writing this book I want to honour and respect the validity of the different learning and assimilation styles of the broad cross-section of individuals to whom I am confident the title has

appeal.

I am encouraging you to practice meditation and journaling. You will greatly benefit from documenting, reflecting and intentionally tracking all matters, which you say are important to you.

To support you in this practice, there are various opportunities for self-evaluation throughout this book with some space provided for documenting your own insights. I hope that you will be inspired with such a flood of insights that you will be moved to utilise a journal or some computer software or some other tool as the dedicated personal record for documenting your insights and documenting other significant matters in your life.

Additionally I am encouraging you not to merely accept things as they appear but to critically think about and evaluate situations for yourself and arrive at your own conclusions. Throughout the book you will therefore find a lot of questions meant to prompt you into this mode of self-examination and critical thinking.

This utility guide and workbook is laid out in two progressive phases.

Phase#1 is what I term "Awaken To ……."；

Phase#2 is what I term "Stay Awake ……."

In the "Awaken To ……." phase I present concepts, tools and practices which I believe once assimilated and put into practice, will enhance individuals progression along a clear pathway towards a fulfilling life.

In the "Stay Awake ……." phase I present scenarios and activities to support individuals in further assimilating the concepts, tools and practices in this book.

Some of you reading this book will enjoy the process of slowly working through it systematically from start to finish; pausing frequently for reflection and documentation of insights and commitments to yourself as you progress through the material. Others of you may prefer to have a quick read of the entire material getting a feel for the key message(s). At a later date you may return to more intentionally work through elements within the book which are of special

appeal. Yet others of you may prefer to get key messages without

all the context.

With all these in mind, I have included two additional areas in this

book.

- **Definitions**[1] to clarify my intended meaning of words that

   may be open to alternative interpretations.

- The **Executive Summary**[2] to succinctly present key messages.

---

[1] PLEASE REFER TO CHAPTER2
[2] PLEASE REFER TO CHAPTER3

Whatever your preferred style I encourage you to have fun with this book. The intention of this utility guide is to offer you a simple proven system that can be duplicated. Yet a system that challenges you to:-

- create your INNER Space For More Personal Evolution;

- personalise Universal Wisdom ;

- be authentic, be you;

- be consciously aware of seven aspects of living and being;

- desire a harmonious life;

- reawaken your sense of self-worth;

- experience a sense of overflowing abundance, peace and joy;

- have a fulfilling life;

- And YES WE CHALLENGE YOU TO **JSRN**, JUST START RIGHT NOW WITH WHAT YOU HAVE.

Commit to yourself to make the best use of this programme and reveal the gems you may have been allowing to rest dormant deep in your heart for a very long time. JSRN! JUST START RIGHT NOW! Stretch if you must and take up the challenge to document and track your personal journey, insights and experiences as you work through the programme and utilise the

harmometer® [3].

You never know. What if your own documented material became a

#1 best seller?

What if your documented personal journey became the basis for a

movie manuscript? Pause and picture this possibility for a

moment; your documented personal journey while working this

JSRN program becoming a best seller; and a movie manuscript.

How would that feel for you? What would your life be like? How

would you be living? Well JUST START RIGHT NOW WITH

WHAT YOU HAVE and you may achieve more that you could

even imagine.

If you were to be the author of such a best seller what would you

want the title to be? Dream for a moment and just write the first

idea that pops in your mind in the space below.

"...

...."

---

[3] PLEASE REFER TO CHAPTER 2.1 FOR A DEFINITION OF
HARMOMETER ®

As you work through this program I encourage you to simply be honest with yourself. Take stock of where you are and what you have right now. As you use the harmometer® and systems presented in this book, expect to accelerate along your personal pathway towards living a fulfilling life. Expect to find new and renewable energy supply. Energy to sustain you as you passionately do the things near and dear to you. Energy to revitalise dreams you had previously buried. Energy to move beyond the past pain, hurts, fears and doubts. Energy to disregard all the nay sayers. Energy to keep on keeping on. But it is important that you JSRN -----Just Start Right Now with what you have!!!.

You may choose to simply work the program from start to finish; or you may skip to the chapter that appeals to you the most. But JSRN !!!! Just Start Right Now….. and have fun working through the rest of this programme.

DEFINITIONS

2. Definitions

2.1. HARMOMETER ®

This is a tool I created for individuals to use as a personal METER for measuring the level of energy and HARMONY in their life. In this book it is presented in the format of a flash card. Please refer to chapter 4 for a more complete discussion of this tool. See also your own copies of the harmometer ® included herein so that you can easily refer to it as you work through the book; keep a copy in your wallet or purse for easy reference during daily activities and share a copy with someone you care about.

2.2. SPIRIT

That invisible, divine realm in which all the potentiality for utmost good for all concerned resides; a realm of all knowledge and all power; a realm of unconditional love; a realm of oneness. The realm many persons have started to intentionally enter in those times when they are seeking

inspiration, peace, joy, harmony and clarity.

2.3. SOUL

For the purpose of this programme, when I use the word "soul"

I am referring to the entire embodiment of **three levels of**

mind action through which we develop, assimilate and

activate our awareness of spirit, awareness of self, and

awareness of the world in which we live. It is through the soul

that we evolve beyond the limits of the physical brain in our

heads as we perceive spiritual and worldly things and make our

choices.

These **three levels of mind action** are (i) the Super-Conscious Mind; (ii) the Conscious Mind; and (iii) the Sub-Conscious Mind.

The Super-Conscious Mind when activated pulls in information from the Spirit.

The Conscious Mind analyses and evaluates information it pulls in from the super-conscious mind, the sub-conscious mind and the five senses as we interact in the world.

The Sub-Conscious Mind records and stores all our decisions, beliefs and emotions.

EXECUTIVE SUMMARY

3. Executive Summary

This book is a project that has evolved out of a personal journey. The book itself is a part of that journey and indeed the personal journey will continue well beyond the publishing of this book. The book incorporates the learnings of a man born and bred in the beautiful Caribbean Island of Jamaica; moi. It takes account of my experiences during world travels across Europe, Indian Ocean Islands, North America and the Caribbean. Over twenty-six years personal experience in the business world spanning sectors including Auditing, Banking, Investing, Stock Broking, Manufacturing, Property Development and Management, Trading, Fast Food, Telecommunication, Wellness and Spirituality have impacted the material incorporated in this book. Twenty years of married life has had a profound effect on perspectives presented in this book. So too has the adjustments necessary in relating with one daughter passing the 18 year old threshold and commencing university life while the other daughter energetically and self-confidently establishes her level of independence at 6 years old.

All these have been tempered by a commitment to a personal

spiritual path. It is out of all of the above along with the related

interactions with hundreds if not thousands of individuals as well

as a realisation that many persons are on a personal search for a

system that is easy to understand and apply that I now present the

material contained in this book. Yes I know, believe and declare

that you can, we all can LIVE A FULFILLING LIFE!!!

The essential idea driving this project is that every individual on

the face of this earth can live a healthy, happy and prosperous life;

if we could just get started right now with what we have.

3.1. JUST START RIGHT NOW WITH WHAT YOU HAVE

Out of the multiplicity of experiences and interactions I have

had, it is clear to me that often times we all have fantastic ideas

and great potential. Ideas, which if acted upon and

implemented, would have had tremendous positive impact not

only on the individual in question who had the idea, but also on

the community and world at large. However, for many varied

reasons, several individuals

remain stuck, do not realise their full potential and just do not

act on or implement the fantastic ideas they have. I am now

offering such persons an opportunity to become unstuck. An

opportunity to; "Just start right now with what you have" and

move towards realising your full potential. This entire book is

based on the application of a simple three-step harmony

formula and the utility of a self-assessment tool that I have

created called the [4]harmometer ® to support the process.

---

[4] REFER TO CHAPTER 2.1 FOR A DEFINITION OF HARMOMETER®

The three-step harmony formula

> **"Being Clear on" (Who I am + My Life Purpose) + Taking Harmonious Actions = Pathway to a Fulfilling Life**

This formula is very simple to recall, is it not? Look at it again, I am sure you can agree.

Both the challenge and victory for us is to consistently apply each element of this formula in our daily life.

Step 1 -"Being clear on Who I am" is a personalised challenge. It seeks to stimulate you to get beyond variable self-definitions associated with the different roles in which you find yourself and encourages you to find new stable definitions that look to the core of your being.

Step 2 "Being clear on My life purpose" is another personalised challenge. This follows on from the first challenge of step 1 and requires you to reassess and define your life purpose given your "new" personalised definition of "Who I am".

Both these challenges start with "Being Clear". This is because the book is encouraging you to focus on your attaining clarity not mere activity in and of itself. We anticipate much inner reflection being

necessary in this area. Do take the time necessary for

reflection on these first two challenges in the formula.

Step 3 "Taking harmonious actions" is the third challenge of

the 3-step harmony formula. Here we encourage you to be and

to remain energised about your life purpose by taking actions

that not only support your life purpose but additionally to take

actions that are in alignment with who you now say you are

and actions that harmonise the seven different aspects of living

and being which we present for your consideration[5] .

In the "Awaken To ...." phase of this book we present

concepts and techniques to support your attaining this clarity.

Additionally the **harmometer** ®[6] is presented in this phase of

the book as a self-assessment tool to gauge your individual

energy and harmony level; the knowledge of which we expect

will guide you to take appropriate remedial actions.

---

[5] PLEASE REFER TO CHAPTER 5.3.1 FOR A FULL DISCUSSION ON THE
SEVEN ASPECTS OF BEING
[6] REFER TO CHAPTER 2.1 FOR A DEFINITION OF HARMOMETER®

In the next phase of this book, the "Stay Awake ...." phase,

we present five generic scenarios in which the material in

phase 1 is effectively applied.

- General interpersonal relationships (key=know

  yourself)

- Credit card debt (key=stay true to your purpose)

- Conflict resolution (key=listening and speaking from

  the heart and feeling nature)

- Money and investing (key=apply the 70:30 & S.I.T

  guidelines and trust yourself)

- Sex (key=being intimate beyond the physical)

As you work with the material in this book we welcome your

feedback and testimonials.

Create or join the conversation on facebook at

fb.me/7quotientsspace4more or

on Instagram at @7quotientsspace4more

Now it is all up to you to choose to get on your pathway to Live a

Fulfilling Life by applying the 3-step harmony formula and

utilising the **harmometer** ® presented in this book.

"Being Clear on" (Who I am + My Life Purpose) + Taking Harmonious Actions

= Pathway to a Fulfilling Life

THE HARMOMETER

4. The Harmometer ®

Today many of us know that the thermometer was created to measure temperature; i.e. a meter for measuring temperature. This basic tool supports us in areas such as personal health care, meal preparation, setting comfortable room temperatures, and scientific experimentation. In each case some kind of criteria can be correlated with the temperature scale, and appropriate actions can be established to be taken given the reading on the temperature scale.

Harmometer ® is a word I created by combining elements of two words, HARMONY and THERMOMETER. It is the name for a tool I created for individuals to use as a personal METER for measuring the level of energy and HARMONY in their life. The [7]**h armometer®** consists of three key areas; **Criteria, Meter, Action**. There is also an interactive area within which you are intended to check-off your personal scale/score for each of the criteria.

[7] KEEP YOUR PERSONAL COPY OF THE HARMOMETER® IN HAND FOR EASY REFERENCE

The criteria I present for consideration in the harmometer ® is

Seven Aspects of Being[8] . These are seven areas I am suggesting

need to be harmonised in each individual's life.

The meter consists of a five-level scale/score system; ranging

from 1 – 5. The lowest scale/score is 1, the highest is 5 with 3

being the "action-trigger" indicator. The aim is to maintain the

harmometer ® scale/score in the 3-5 range. Corrective actions are

necessary whenever the harmometer ® scale/score is less than 3.

In the case of [9]**investment actions**, the percentages presented at

the bottom of each scale are the suggested percent of your funds to

be expended.

---

[8] PLEASE REFER TO CHAPTER 5.3.1 FOR A FULL DISCUSSION ON
SEVEN ASPECTS OF BEING
[9] PLEASE REFER TO CHAPTER 6.1.4 FOR A CASE STUDY IN THIS
AREA.

PERSONAL HARMOMETER® (pH)
When I Get Still And Reflect On Each Of These 7-Aspects
Of Being FROM MY HEART, I Feel :-

7 ASPECTS OF BEING:-	Entirely Depleted 1	Low 2	Average 3	High 4	Fully Elevated 5
SPIRITUAL					
MENTAL / EMOTIONAL					
PHYSICAL					
RELATIONAL					
SOCIAL					
VOCATIONAL					
FINANCIAL					
% TO EXPEND	0%	25%	50%	75%	100%

PAUL ANTHONY EDWARDS - EMAIL: 7QUOTIENTS@GMAIL.COM FOR PERMISSION
©2004-2017

USE THE PERSONAL HARMOMETER

*PROACTIVELY >>>	TO STAY AWARE OF YOUR PERSONAL STATE OF HARMONY OVER 7 DIFFERENT BUT RELATED PARAMETERS
*REACTIVELY >>>	TO EVALUATE THE IMPACT OF AN EVENT/INTERACTION ON YOUR STATE OF HARMONY
*INTENTIONALLY >>>	TO SET THE DESIRED OUTCOME, OF A PLANNED INTERACTION, FOR YOU AND THE OTHER PARTIES
*STRATEGICALLY >>>	TO IDENTIFY YOUR KEY ENERGY DRIVER OUT OF THE SEVEN ASPECTS OF BEING LISTED
*DAILY >>>	TO SEE WHICH OF THE 7 ASPECTS OF BEING IS CRYING OUT FOR FOCUSSED ATTENTION

RECALL THAT THE SCALE/SCORE RANGE OF 1 - 5 IS WHAT YOU USE TO RANK EACH OF THE 7-ASPECTS OF BEING. THE SCORE OF 3 IS THE TRIGGER POINT FOR ACTION; ANY ITEM WITH A SCORE LESS THAN 3 NEEDS AN ACTION PLAN FOR CORRECTIVE STEP(S) TO STIMULATE YOU TO TREND TOWARDS A SCORE OF 4 >>> 5

7QUOTIENTS - CALL +1(876)289-4874 - UNIT#1 10 ELLESMERE DRIVE, KINGSTON 19, JAMAICA

Note to reader: Cut out this entire leaf, laminate, then cut down to 3 credit-card size cards

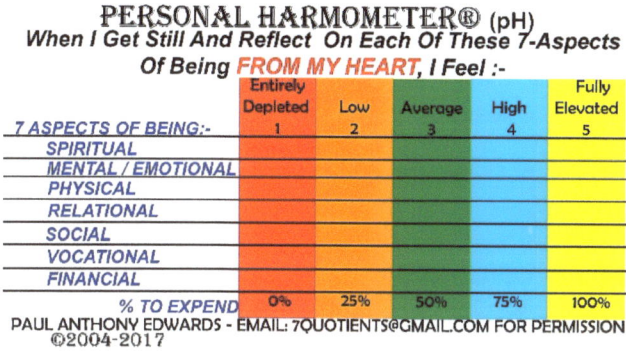

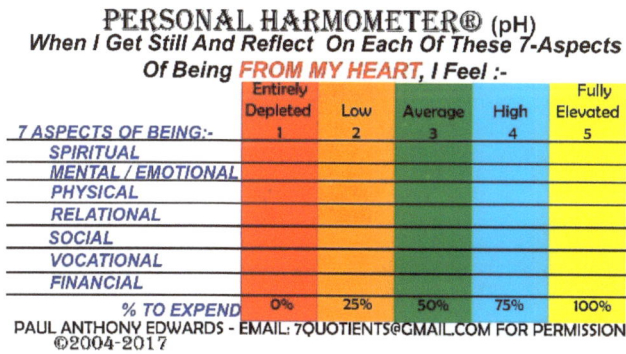

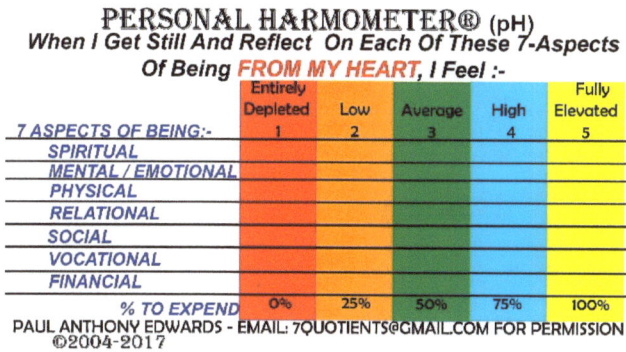

PERSONAL HARMOMETER® (pH)
When I Get Still And Reflect On Each Of These 7-Aspects Of Being FROM MY HEART*, I Feel :-*

7 ASPECTS OF BEING:-	Entirely Depleted 1	Low 2	Average 3	High 4	Fully Elevated 5
SPIRITUAL					
MENTAL / EMOTIONAL					
PHYSICAL					
RELATIONAL					
SOCIAL					
VOCATIONAL					
FINANCIAL					
% TO EXPEND	0%	25%	50%	75%	100%

PAUL ANTHONY EDWARDS - EMAIL: 7QUOTIENTS@GMAIL.COM FOR PERMISSION
©2004-2017

PERSONAL HARMOMETER® (pH)
When I Get Still And Reflect On Each Of These 7-Aspects Of Being FROM MY HEART*, I Feel :-*

7 ASPECTS OF BEING:-	Entirely Depleted 1	Low 2	Average 3	High 4	Fully Elevated 5
SPIRITUAL					
MENTAL / EMOTIONAL					
PHYSICAL					
RELATIONAL					
SOCIAL					
VOCATIONAL					
FINANCIAL					
% TO EXPEND	0%	25%	50%	75%	100%

PAUL ANTHONY EDWARDS - EMAIL: 7QUOTIENTS@GMAIL.COM FOR PERMISSION
©2004-2017

PERSONAL HARMOMETER® (pH)
When I Get Still And Reflect On Each Of These 7-Aspects Of Being FROM MY HEART*, I Feel :-*

7 ASPECTS OF BEING:-	Entirely Depleted 1	Low 2	Average 3	High 4	Fully Elevated 5
SPIRITUAL					
MENTAL / EMOTIONAL					
PHYSICAL					
RELATIONAL					
SOCIAL					
VOCATIONAL					
FINANCIAL					
% TO EXPEND	0%	25%	50%	75%	100%

PAUL ANTHONY EDWARDS - EMAIL: 7QUOTIENTS@GMAIL.COM FOR PERMISSION
©2004-2017

USE THE PERSONAL HARMOMETER

*PROACTIVELY >>>	TO STAY AWARE OF YOUR PERSONAL STATE OF HARMONY OVER 7 DIFFERENT BUT RELATED PARAMETERS
*REACTIVELY >>>	TO EVALUATE THE IMPACT OF AN EVENT/INTERACTION ON YOUR STATE OF HARMONY
*INTENTIONALLY >>>	TO SET THE DESIRED OUTCOME, OF A PLANNED INTERACTION, FOR YOU AND THE OTHER PARTIES
*STRATEGICALLY >>>	TO IDENTIFY YOUR KEY ENERGY DRIVER OUT OF THE SEVEN ASPECTS OF BEING LISTED
*DAILY >>>	TO SEE WHICH OF THE 7 ASPECTS OF BEING IS CRYING OUT FOR FOCUSSED ATTENTION

RECALL THAT THE SCALE/SCORE RANGE OF 1 - 5 IS WHAT YOU USE TO RANK EACH OF THE 7 ASPECTS OF BEING. THE SCORE OF 3 IS THE TRIGGER POINT FOR ACTION; ANY ITEM WITH A SCORE LESS THAN 3 NEEDS AN ACTION PLAN FOR CORRECTIVE STEP(S) TO STIMULATE YOU TO TREND TOWARDS A SCORE OF 4 >>> 5

7QUOTIENTS - CALL +1(876)289-4874 - UNIT#1 10 ELLESMERE DRIVE, KINGSTON 19, JAMAICA

USE THE PERSONAL HARMOMETER

*PROACTIVELY >>>	TO STAY AWARE OF YOUR PERSONAL STATE OF HARMONY OVER 7 DIFFERENT BUT RELATED PARAMETERS
*REACTIVELY >>>	TO EVALUATE THE IMPACT OF AN EVENT/INTERACTION ON YOUR STATE OF HARMONY
*INTENTIONALLY >>>	TO SET THE DESIRED OUTCOME, OF A PLANNED INTERACTION, FOR YOU AND THE OTHER PARTIES
*STRATEGICALLY >>>	TO IDENTIFY YOUR KEY ENERGY DRIVER OUT OF THE SEVEN ASPECTS OF BEING LISTED
*DAILY >>>	TO SEE WHICH OF THE 7 ASPECTS OF BEING IS CRYING OUT FOR FOCUSSED ATTENTION

RECALL THAT THE SCALE/SCORE RANGE OF 1 - 5 IS WHAT YOU USE TO RANK EACH OF THE 7 ASPECTS OF BEING. THE SCORE OF 3 IS THE TRIGGER POINT FOR ACTION; ANY ITEM WITH A SCORE LESS THAN 3 NEEDS AN ACTION PLAN FOR CORRECTIVE STEP(S) TO STIMULATE YOU TO TREND TOWARDS A SCORE OF 4 >>> 5

7QUOTIENTS - CALL +1(876)289-4874 - UNIT#1 10 ELLESMERE DRIVE, KINGSTON 19, JAMAICA

USE THE PERSONAL HARMOMETER

*PROACTIVELY >>>	TO STAY AWARE OF YOUR PERSONAL STATE OF HARMONY OVER 7 DIFFERENT BUT RELATED PARAMETERS
*REACTIVELY >>>	TO EVALUATE THE IMPACT OF AN EVENT/INTERACTION ON YOUR STATE OF HARMONY
*INTENTIONALLY >>>	TO SET THE DESIRED OUTCOME, OF A PLANNED INTERACTION, FOR YOU AND THE OTHER PARTIES
*STRATEGICALLY >>>	TO IDENTIFY YOUR KEY ENERGY DRIVER OUT OF THE SEVEN ASPECTS OF BEING LISTED
*DAILY >>>	TO SEE WHICH OF THE 7 ASPECTS OF BEING IS CRYING OUT FOR FOCUSSED ATTENTION

RECALL THAT THE SCALE/SCORE RANGE OF 1 - 5 IS WHAT YOU USE TO RANK EACH OF THE 7 ASPECTS OF BEING. THE SCORE OF 3 IS THE TRIGGER POINT FOR ACTION; ANY ITEM WITH A SCORE LESS THAN 3 NEEDS AN ACTION PLAN FOR CORRECTIVE STEP(S) TO STIMULATE YOU TO TREND TOWARDS A SCORE OF 4 >>> 5

7QUOTIENTS - CALL +1(876)289-4874 - UNIT#1 10 ELLESMERE DRIVE, KINGSTON 19, JAMAICA

PHASE#1 – AWAKEN TO …

AWAKEN TO A THREE STEP HARMONY FORMULA

5.1. AWAKEN TO A THREE STEP HARMONY

FORMULA

"Being Clear on" (Who I am + My Life Purpose) + Taking Harmonious Actions = Pathway to a Fulfilling Life

The formula highlighted in the box above is presented in the format $x(A+B) + C = D$.

Recall also the mathematical principle of solving the elements within the brackets first, before completing the remainder of the formula. Also recall that the "x" factor influences everything within the brackets. I challenge you to work with the formula above and prove its validity with your life experience.

27

Ponder and reflect on the following three simple personalized questions:

  1. Who am I?

  2. What is my life purpose?

  3. Are all my actions in alignment with 1 & 2? Are my actions in harmony?

We each have different knowledge, skills, abilities and a multitude of natural gifts and talents. The question is what are we doing with them? What reason have we given ourselves to stimulate ourselves to consistently make the highest and best use of all of this "stuff" that is uniquely us? Can you imagine what this world would be like if every individual on the face of the Earth had clear answers to each of the above three questions. Even better, what if everyone was acting upon those answers consistently and with integrity? Do you have clear answers for yourself to each question above?

Which approach would be more powerful; (i) Asking someone to tell you the answers relevant for you or (ii) Perceiving the answers for yourself?

Pause for a moment and take some quality time to reflect on all of the above things and document your insights.

It is often suggested that our inner circle of friends see the possibilities for us probably even clearer than we see them for ourselves. There is some truth in this.

However, there is yet another truth, the awareness of which allows us to be more in alignment with our true nature, and which empowers us to be even more perceptive.

5.2. AWAKEN TO YOUR THREE-FOLD NATURE

Agree with me if you will that all of us are of a three-fold nature. Each of these three elements, a crucial element which combines to form the unique individual we each are. None of which, however, can exist as the "all" of us by itself. Some of which we may deny any importance. All of which we take with us wherever we are. Much of which is winning increasing amounts of Radio and TV airtime. All of which is being included in everyday discussions more and more. What are the elements of this three-fold nature?

- [10]Spirit

- [11]Soul/Mind

- Body

In this view of man's true make-up there is an optimal flow from ideas through to action where the ideas are first accessed from spirit; analysed, evaluated, decided on and stored by the soul/mind; which then influences the activities undertaken in

---

[10] PLEASE REFER TO DEFINITION 2.2
[11] PLEASE REFER TO DEFINITION 2.3

the world of our five senses, called the <u>body</u> in this context.

There is also a sub-optimal flow of ideas and action. This is where the spiritual realm is subrogated (knowingly or unknowingly) and greater credence placed upon ideas accessed from the popular belief system of the community; called the race consciousness. This race consciousness is then accepted and stored by the soul/mind; which then influences the activities undertaken in the body of this world on the level of the five senses.

The key to note is that the process of man's 3-fold nature works every time whether we allow it to be fed with ideas from spirit or with ideas from the community/race consciousness.

Idea-processed by the soul-leads to action in the body of this world.

If this three-fold nature is true then there is a common basis from which we can all answer question 1 of the "harmony formula" above: 1. Who am I? We now have an opportunity to move away from self-definitions that vary in accordance with the particular role we find ourselves in or perceive ourselves as being in. We now have an opportunity to create new self-definitions focused on the stable 3-fold nature/core of ourselves.

Pause, ponder and document your "new" self-definition.

Now what of the other two questions of the "harmony formula":

2. What is my **life purpose**?

3. Are all my **actions in alignment** with 1 & 2? Are my **actions in harmony**?

Humankind: A 3-Fold Being
(Spirit, Soul, Body)

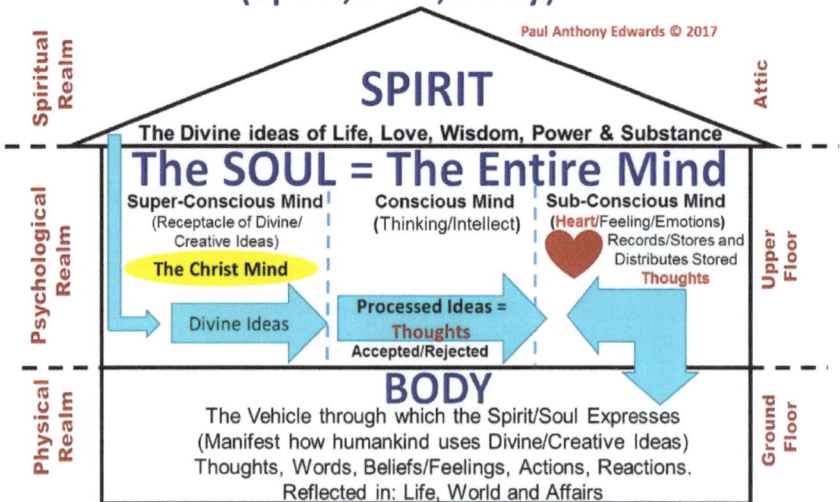

Paul Anthony Edwards © 2017

Spiritual Realm — **Attic**

SPIRIT
The Divine ideas of Life, Love, Wisdom, Power & Substance

The SOUL = The Entire Mind

Psychological Realm — **Upper Floor**

Super-Conscious Mind (Receptacle of Divine/ Creative Ideas) — **The Christ Mind**

Conscious Mind (Thinking/Intellect)

Sub-Conscious Mind (Heart/Feeling/Emotions) Records/Stores and Distributes Stored Thoughts

Divine Ideas

Processed Ideas = Thoughts Accepted/Rejected

Physical Realm — **Ground Floor**

BODY
The Vehicle through which the Spirit/Soul Expresses (Manifest how humankind uses Divine/Creative Ideas) Thoughts, Words, Beliefs/Feelings, Actions, Reactions. Reflected in: Life, World and Affairs

5.3. AWAKEN TO ALL OF YOU

5.3.1. BE CONSCIOUS OF ALL SEVEN ASPECTS OF LIVING AND BEING

We all get caught up in the business of daily life in the 21st century, racing the clock, attending to such things as learning academic material; preparing for and sitting exams; meeting deadlines; achieving work objectives established by our bosses; keeping businesses afloat; job hunting; surviving; making money; providing clothing, food, transportation and shelter; paying bills; being a good father, mother, care-giver, spouse, sister, brother, friend, lover; looking good; to name a few. We all perceive that getting up in the morning, taking care of hygiene matters, and attending to the above type of daily routine, will of itself, be insufficient to attain a sense of living life harmoniously, of living a fulfilling life. Yet many of us cannot seem to get off this treadmill of life.

Reach for your own copy of the harmometer®, which is a tool I am recommending that you work with. By so doing, it is my belief that you will be informed of seven aspects of living and being that need appropriate focus and attention. You will gain knowledge of where that illusive void lies. You will assimilate the simple mechanism incorporated within this tool, designed to help you identify any gaps in your life. You may even gain new/renewed insights on a sense of purpose. We are actually multidimensional beings capable of appreciating and treating all seven aspects of being consciously. We can awake to the fact that up to now, the interplay between all seven aspects of being may have eluded our conscious awareness. NO MORE!!!!

The seven aspects of being are:-

1. Spiritual - which keeps us in tune with universal, divine intelligence, the realm of all potentiality for utmost good for all concerned. What I have come to view as the real core of our being.

2. Emotional/Mental -which is where our perceiving, thinking, feeling and reasoning nature lie.

3. Physical – which is where we interact with the three-dimensional world from the point of our five senses; see, touch, hear, smell, taste. The focus here is on our general wellness.

4. Relational – which is where our interpersonal communication, our "one-to-one" relationships play out

5. Social - which is where communication with a community, our "one-to-many" relationships play out

6. Vocational aspect of being which is concerned with our calling towards a particular occupation (student, employee, retiree, business owner etc)

7. Financial aspect of being which is simply concerned about our money matters

ACTIVITY 1

Take your copy of the harmometer ® and ponder these seven aspects of being in your special quiet place free from all distractions. Take a diary (or simply cut an exercise book in half) and pencil with you. Document and date your insights, revelations and commitments to yourself. Note that there are blank pages to the back of this book to facilitate your starting this documenting process. Consider the following questions:

1.1 Does any of the seven have a special appeal to you? Why?

1.2 Is there any aspect of being that you have been overlooking? Why?

1.3 Which one of these seven aspects of being will you give focused attention over the next week? What specific actions will you take to grow in this area? At what specific time of day? How much time will you commit to this each day over this next week? [We are saying a week so that you can just get started right now.]

1.4 What changes do you expect as a result of taking these actions?

1.5 Do you perceive your life purpose and any alignment with any of these areas of being? Write it down, meditate on it, and see what plans are revealed and evolve over time.

1.6 Can you perceive how the seven aspects of being interplay with each other in your own life, world and affairs?

After the first week, check your level of accomplishment against the commitment you had made to yourself and then take a week off. Repeat the exercise thereafter as often as there is a felt need; seeing areas of improvement and seeing if a different aspect of being tugs for attention

So now you may be thinking, "OK I can appreciate how the harmometer ® can enhance my conscious awareness of the seven aspects of living and being. I can even concede that it helps me clarify my life purpose. But what about question 3 in the three step formula – **Harmonious actions**?"

5.4. AWAKEN TO INVISIBLE ENERGY FLOWS

5.4.1. BE CONSCIOUS OF YOUR ENERGY LEVEL

Any action, to be sustained, requires energy. Alignment with **life purpose** gives motivation, a reason for action. It is, however, high energy that ensures consistency of action. At some point in our life we have heard the statement "Energy is neither created nor destroyed it merely changes from one state to another". We, however, may not have applied this to our own internal energy systems neither to the transfer of energy between each aspect of being nor even to the transfer of energy between persons during any interaction. With the harmometer ® there is a simple scale/scoring system to rank your own internal energy level for each of the seven aspects of being. Additionally, the same scoring system can be used to evaluate the impact any interaction had or is likely to have on your own energy system.

The harmometer ®scale is shown in the following table

ENTIRELY DEPLETED	LOW	AVERAGE	HIGH	FULLY ELEVATED
1	2	3	4	5

If you had to choose to open one of the two doors below to interact with a group of people who would support you as you evolve to higher heights, being a more authentic you, which door would you choose?

Door#1 leads to a room full of non-achievers, nay sayers, believing in doom and gloom, all with their energy levels entirely depleted, and generally an air of hopelessness prevails.

Door#5 leads to a room of high-achievers, sharing their knowledge, skills & ability with each other, seeking additional opportunities, all with their energy levels fully elevated, and generally an air of having fun, a sense of oneness and an "I can attitude" prevails.

Each room is a depiction of you, depending on the energy level of and interplay between each of your seven aspects of being.

Let us agree then that the intention is to maintain our energy levels on the harmometer ® scale at 3 or above. Additionally, let us recognize the signal that there is need for appropriate corrective steps to be taken whenever the scale is at a score less than 3.

ACTIVITY 2

Set aside some time to be alone in your special quiet place free from all distractions. Take a diary (or simply cut an exercise book in half) and pencil with you. Document and date your insights, revelations and commitments to yourself. From the harmometer ® :

2.1 Consider the spiritual aspect of being and imagine that your energy level is at its lowest -entirely depleted (a score of 1). When you are in this "entirely depleted" space spiritually, consider in turn its impact on each of the other six aspects of being?

2.2 Now imagine that the energy level for your spiritual aspect of being changes to its highest – fully elevated (a score of 5). What can you see in your mind's eye happening to the energy levels in the other six aspects of being?

2.3 Now take the emotional aspect of being and repeat the exercise first with the energy level being at its lowest, then changing to its highest as above.

2.4 Keep repeating the exercise using each of the remaining five aspects of being in turn.

2.5 Do you have any new insights/revelations on the interconnectivity between the seven aspects of being as a result of this exercise?

2.6 Have you identified any one aspect that has the greatest influence on all the others for you?

2.7 How are you going to use these insights/revelations to positively influence your life?

2.8 What commitments are you willing to make to yourself in this regard?

We have now completed phase#1 of the program, the "Awaken to …." phase. We are now intimate with the [12]**harmometer**® and the **3-step harmony formula**[13]. We now know how critical it is to stay in alignment with our **3-fold nature**[14] in order to have optimal results. We are clear that we are multidimensional, that there are **seven aspects of living & being, and that energy is transmitted between each**[15].

Now its time to "**Stay Awake**………." and consistently utilize this knowledge to its fullest advantage in our everyday life, world and affairs.

---

[12] Please refer to chapter 4
[13] Please refer to chapter 5.1
[14] Please refer to chapter 5.2
[15] Please refer to chapter 5.3 to 5.4

PHASE#2 – STAY AWAKE

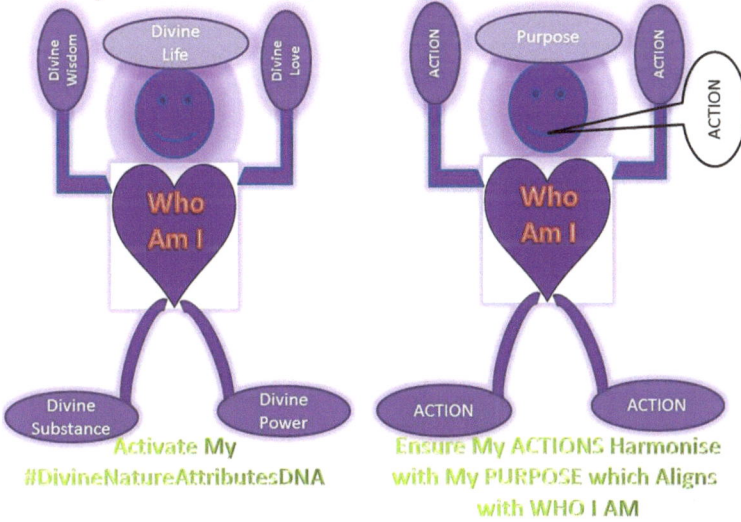

43

6.1. STAY AWAKE AND MAKE CONSCIOUS CHOICES

By keeping the [16]**harmometer** ® close at hand you can quickly evaluate your energy and harmony levels in various every day scenarios and choose the most harmonious action that is right for you. Just start right now with what you have, "new knowledge & information", and consistently apply this knowledge to its fullest advantage in your everyday life, world and affairs. This next phase, phase#2, looks at some practical applications.

---

[16] Please pull your copy of the personal **harmometer** ® and dive into the conscious choice of your preference that follows

CONSCIOUS CHOICE – ATTRACTING RELATIONSHIPS

THAT WORK

6.1.1. CONSCIOUS CHOICE - ATTRACTING

RELATIONSHIPS THAT WORK

Are you ready to deal with relationships that work?
Are you ready to guard against relationships which are
allowed to evolve to the level of addictive co-
dependencies? Addictions, which lead to us acting
crazy and making inappropriate choices? There are
many positive attributes of relationships in which co-
dependencies are freely displayed; you support and
care for me; I support and care for you. The caution,
however, is to guard against such relationships
evolving to an addictive state.

We all are aware of the self-destructive actions of a drug addict and the withdrawal symptoms displayed when the next "fix" is not available or is even perceived to be withheld. Not many of us, however, are conscious of such addictions in relationships even though similar withdrawal symptoms are often displayed right in front of our own eyes. There are other possibilities. Imagine with me, a time when and a place where we are all involved only in relationships that remind us of how special we are; that clarify and support our dreams; that energise and uplift us; that stimulate our awareness of even greater possibilities for our lives. In your mind's eye, see yourself living in such a place and time. What are you being and how are you feeling in that place and time? This can be your reality right now and the **harmometer** ® can be a supporting tool in the process.

Pause for a moment and take some quality time to reflect on these things and document your insights.

6.1.1.1. "HOOK UP" ONLY AFTER YOU

TRULY KNOW YOURSELF

In these modern times we need to balance the media messages of instant gratification with a more holistic approach. An approach that encourages individuals to seek out relationships with others (or "hook up") only after they have first clarified their relationship with themselves. This approach activates the law of attraction which states that; **"you draw to yourself what you are being"**.

If you are being fearful, then relationships and life experiences that are in alignment with your fearful state cannot help but be attracted to you. If you are angry at the world then it should be no surprise when experiences that feed your anger are attracted to you. It is simply the law of attraction in action.

Since this law of attraction is just that, "a law" why not invoke it powerfully? Why not put it to the test and start observing the

47

relationships and life experiences that you attract when

you intentionally practice new approaches to self-

awareness, living and being?

Commit then to (a) activate the three-step formula[17] (b)

spend daily quiet time for reflection with yourself.

Contemplate your three-fold nature[18] and your seven

aspects of living and being[19] (c) continually remind

yourself of your inner energy supply. Meditate on the

free flow of this source of energy and awaken to your

own invisible source of energy flows[20].

---

[17] Please refer to chapter 5.1
[18] Please refer to chapter 5.2
[19] Please refer to chapter 5.3.1
[20] Please refer to chapter 5.4.1

CONSCIOUS CHOICE – DOMINION OVER CREDIT CARD
DEBTS

6.1.2. CONSCIOUS CHOICE – DOMINION OVER CREDIT CARD DEBTS

Jean-Luke has recently cleared all his credit card debts by taking out a Credit Union loan and paying all the cards off. He now has one low interest rate loan that will be fully paid off in five years.

He also gained the understanding that unsecured loans (such as credit card debt) can be utilized effectively to take advantage of business opportunities. The key is to ensure that the "business" can earn enough to pay off the loan plus interest and leave a surplus. Jean-Luke learned that this activity is called ….. **LEVERAGING DEBT**. As such he decided to exercise dominion over his credit cards. He chose not to cut them up but instead has set the intention to utilise them only for business opportunities or pay them off monthly if used for consumables.

Jean-Luke's challenge is that he likes to entertain and support family and friends, often times beyond his income or inflows. In the past he paid for these bills with his credit cards, which slowly lead to the buildup of his credit card debt. He has decided to take control. Consequently many opportunities arise that support him in this regard. One such scenario follows below.

Now Jean-Luke has clean credit cards with zero balances; a family member asks for his support in settling a bill she has. Jean-Luke has no surplus income to facilitate this. What should he do? Stop...... Don't go unconscious, acting as if on autopilot and pay the bill as he did previously with his credit card. Instead Jean-Luke can first reach for his **harmometer** ® and evaluate the impact of such a decision on all his seven aspects of being. Remembering

that the goal is to maintain the **harmometer** ®

scale reading at 3 or above for all seven aspect of

living and being; he will stay

mindful of the interrelationship between all these 7

aspects of being. He will not "gratify one" at the

expense of others. After evaluating the impact on

his energy levels if he were to make the payment,

he is in a better space to choose the harmonious

action(s) most appropriate given the readings on

the **harmometer** ® scale.

6.1.3. CONSCIOUS CHOICE – RESOLVING CONFLICTS WITHOUT GIVING UP THE TRUE YOU

In situations where there are differences of opinion as to the best action to take; with the [21]**harmometer ®** it is no longer necessary to have discussions, debates, and arguments centered around whose position is right and whose is wrong. Neither will it be sufficient to reach surface level compromises, which leave either party feeling unfulfilled.

Now each party can take equal uninterrupted time in expressing the impact of their actions on all seven aspects of their being while the other party listens holistically. After both parties clearly present their position and appreciate the other party's **harmometer ®** level, next, they can

---

[21] Please refer to chapter 4

consider alternative actions that can be taken so as to push both party's **harmometer** ® scale reading into the upper regions of 3 – 5 [22].

Remember that the **harmometer** ® scale is an indicator of one's energy level which is evaluated based on ones feeling nature in each aspect of being. As such it is vitally important that the listener listens to and does not interrupt the speaker as he/she shares his/her innermost self. It is not necessary or even useful for the listener to give any opinion on what is being said.

The listener is not being asked to agree with what is being said; just breathe deeply, listen and get in tune with the energy and feelings of the speaker. To do otherwise is to miss a great opportunity of enhancing a mutual sense of respect, love and oneness for the other party.

---

[22] Please refer to chapters 5.3 – 5.4

CONSCIOUS CHOICE – TRUST YOURSELF TO MAKE

EFFECTIVE INVESTMENT DECISIONS

6.1.4. CONSCIOUS CHOICE – TRUST YOURSELF TO MAKE EFFECTIVE INVESTMENT DECISIONS

Save Invest and Tithe, and "S.I.T." with the air of authority and dominion of an Egyptian Pharaoh over your financial affairs. This is Sharee's current goal after attending several financial workshops. She is a single mom of two who teaches first graders at a government/public school in the beautiful Caribbean Island of Jamaica. She now knows the **financial independence definition of AN ASSET; "Any item acquired from which positive cash flows (income) are generated".**

She also buys into the 70:30 financial independence

principle of dividing her income. No more than

70% for creating the lifestyle she can enjoy; no less

than 30% towards nurturing her financial

independence by intentionally focusing on the

development of her personal ASSET BASE.

She understands that "S.I.T" forms three distinct

tiers within her ASSET BASE as depicted by

diagram#1 below.

Diagram#1 **The 70:30 S.I.T. Plan**

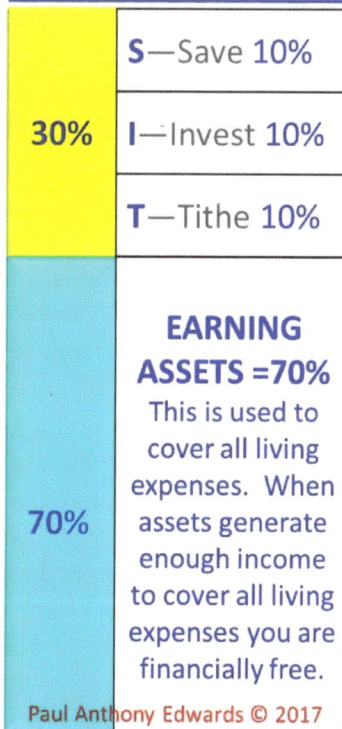

30%	S—Save 10%
	I—Invest 10%
	T—Tithe 10%
70%	**EARNING ASSETS =70%** This is used to cover all living expenses. When assets generate enough income to cover all living expenses you are financially free.

Paul Anthony Edwards © 2017

It is with the 30% income allocation that she develops the consistent habit to S.I.T.

S ave – Is the approach used to create the second tier in her ASSET BASE. Using the second 10% of her income she can create safe ASSETS, which grow minimally in a secure environment (refer to diagram#1 above). The focus of "Saving" is value retention, and loss avoidance.

These safe ASSETS include but are not limited to accounts at Banks, Credit Unions, Building Societies, Money Market Pooled Funds in Government Securities (in stable countries). Further, as she lives in a country where the national currency depreciates steadily versus regional and international currencies; it is prudent to maintain a portion of these savings in strong and stable foreign currency denominated accounts.

I nvest – Is the approach used to create the third and top tier in her personal ASSET BASE. Using the third 10% of her income she can create growth ASSETS, which grow more rapidly than safe Assets (refer to diagram#1 above). The focus of "Investing" is value creation and growth. These growth ASSETS include but are not limited to Stocks, Bonds, Investment Properties and Businesses.

T ithe – Is the approach used to ensure that the first tier of her personal ASSET BASE is divine in nature. Using the first 10% of her income she can contribute to the "Universal Asset Base"(refer to diagram#1 above). This is where Sharee develops the systematic and consistent practice of giving to the organization that feeds her spiritually. It is an acknowledgement that there is a "Universal Asset Base" the source of which is divine in nature and the supply of which can never run dry. It is also a practice, which allows her to view her financial matters through the lens of the "big picture perspective"; a picture through which she is reminded that the real source of her supply is divine and unlimited in nature. It is a practice, which facilitates the growth of her faith factor and the belief that she will be guided into right action, during her quiet moments.

When Sharee came upon this 70:30 information she was at a place where her lifestyle was such that she had no personal ASSET BASE, she had expenses equal to 110% of her income and there were constant intense fights with Don, the father of her two children.

It took her three years to rebalance her affairs (lifestyle) and to be able to divide her income 70:30; paying out the cheques for the 30% first before paying any of the bills. This way she put herself and her personal ASSET BASE (S.I.T) first, before any of the suppliers of the products and services she utilizes for herself and her children. She could not start the S.I.T program with 30% of her income as it just was not possible at that time; so she started with Ja$300; Ja$200 to Savings, Ja$0 to Investment and Ja$100 to Tithe. She then revisited her consumption patterns and made necessary adjustments downwards. This meant that she had created more disposable income which she channeled towards Tithing, focusing initially on hitting the "tier one" target by increasing the Ja$100 to 10% of her income. Sharee also flipped the 70:30 guideline on its head, each time it came to annual salary increases and Christmas bonus; in these instances 70% went to S.I.T. and 30% to consumables.

So Sharee reached a place where 30% of her income was allocated to S.I.T. as follows; 20% to Savings, 0% to Investments and 10% to Tithe. Her challenge has been that 20% was placed into tier two of her ASSET BASE -----safe Assets, the Savings element; none was applied into tier three ----growth Assets, the Investment element. Her self-doubt dominated   until she started to

59

utilize the **harmometer** ® and increasingly trusted

herself to make effective investment decisions.

Now, each month, after allocating the 10% for

Investments, see seeks out the best information and

advice. Armed with the amount she has to invest

and the options before her to choose from, she

subjects them to the **harmometer** ® test for all her

seven aspects of being. So now she does not do as

the professional advisors suggest; instead she listens

to the advisors but acts in accordance with

her own inner guide as evaluated with the

harmometer ® (see extract below). When the

harmometer ® registers at the lowest end of the

scale where the reading is a score of 1, then no

investment allocation is made (0%) no matter the

product under consideration. Whereas when the

harmometer ® registers at the highest end of the

scale where the reading is a score of 5, then 100%

of the current dollar allocation for investments are

placed in the product under consideration. An

extract from the **harmometer** ® is below.

	PERSONAL HARMOMETER ®				
	WHEN I CONSIDER MAKING THIS EXPENDITURE, IN MY HEART I FEEL AS IF MY ASPECT OF BEING IS :-				
	1 ENTIRELY DEPLETED	2 LOW	3 NEUTRAL	4 HIGH	5 ENTIRELY UPLIFTED
HARMONIOUS INVESTMENT ACTION = % TO EXPEND	0%	25%	50%	75%	100%

Sharee is now on a clear pathway towards hitting

another financial independence target:-

To generate at least 70% of her income from her

Asset Base.

She has set a Savings target by multiplying 70% of

her **monthly income amount** by 200. She is really

energised about hitting this next target because she

knows that at that point she will be truly financially

free. Free because she would have not only adjusted

her life to live on 70% of her income but at that

point her ASSET BASE will also be providing the

70% of her income.

Can you feel within your soul what it would be like to be in such a place of freedom for yourself?

You can get on this path to financial independence too. Just start right now with what you have.

1st Write down the targets -

70% of your income = _____

30% of you income = _____

2nd Be honest, how does your current spending habit stack up against these targets. Remember no more that 70% for spending/supporting your life style; and no less than 30% for S.I.T. Do not beat upon yourself if you are out of balance with the targets. Just start right now with what you have and make small but consistent adjustments to move yourself closer and closer to the targets. It is a process, be strong and courageous and act in accordance with your new resolve. You can do it. But most importantly, JSRN ….just start right now with what you have.

CONSCIOUS CHOICE – MULTIDIMENSIONAL SEXUAL

FULFILLMENT

6.1.5. **CONSCIOUS CHOICE – MULTI-**

DIMENSIONAL SEXUAL FULFILLMENT

In "this world" it is somewhat common for sexual

fulfillment to be associated with the frequency and

intensity of the ecstatic climax attained between

partners during sexual intercourse. In fact major

commercial industries are prospering through

supporting this limited belief system.

Imagine if you will, that sexual intercourse was an

expression of universal oneness, a coming together

of spirit, soul **then** body, entered into only after

mature and **committed** partners were first

intentionally intimate in all seven aspects of being[23]

.

---

[23] Please refer to chapter 5.3 – 5.4

I dare suggest that the sexual experience under such circumstances would be beyond "this world"; I suggest that what would be experienced is "multidimensional sexual fulfillment".

The harmometer ® is also useful here as it provides an objective communication methodology to take the sexual discussion and ultimately the experience between partners beyond the fault finding, finger pointing, single (physical) dimensional, who is at fault, who wants it too much, who does not want it enough, who is driving whom to seek satisfaction elsewhere, unfulfilling type of sexual intimacy. First partners can use the harmometer ® for support in resolving conflicts[24].

---

[24] Please refer to chapter 6.1.3

Additionally, you can aim for "multidimensional sexual fulfillment". Get honest with yourself; evaluate your current level of intimacy; commit to be changed from the inside out starting with the man or woman in the mirror. By the way, that means start with you!! Perform activity 3 as outlined below. As your level of intimacy increases across all seven aspects of being, expect to experience sexual fulfillment that is beyond "this world".

A big question though is "Do you really want to be intimate at this level with your current partner; the level of being intimate in ALL, yes ALL seven aspects of being?"

HEALTH WARNING – Go and perform activity 3 only if your answer is yes.

ACTIVITY 3

Set aside some time to be alone in your special quiet place free from all distractions. Take a diary (or simply cut an exercise book in half) and pencil with you. Document and date your insights, revelations and commitments to yourself.

3.1 For each of the seven aspects of being use the harmometer ® scale to complete and score the following self-assessment statement, "When I consider the level of intimacy between

my partner and I in this aspect of being, in my heart I feel ……………."
3.2 Do the scores reveal any aspect of being in which there is scope for improvement in intimacy between you and your partner?
3.3 What steps can you intentionally take to be more intimate in this area? List and prioritise them.
3.4 Are there any steps your partner could intentionally take to be more intimate in this area? List and prioritise them.
3.5 If you listed more actions for your partner to take than yourself, (1) revisit your list, be more introspective (2) revisit your partners list and transfer any items that are really indicative of past hurts you are still holding on to, over to your own list. However, restate them on your list as personal intentional actions of forgiveness.
3.6 Be clear on your intention for recording all these action steps.
Do not share any of the above with your partner at this time. It is all about you being clear as to your perspective and your responsibility for the level of intimacy experienced in each aspect of being.

++++++++End this element of the session here++++++++

ACTIVITY 3 Continued

At a later date:

3.7 Let your partner know that you would like to set aside some quality time to discuss a matter that is important to you; at this point you may articulate your intention (refer to 3.6 above)

3.8 During the "quality time" discussion itself:

    3.8.1 Lead off with your intention followed by the steps you are willing to take. Then ask your partner if he/she agrees, or if there are any better steps he/she sees as being possible for you to take to support the stated intention. Once you have agreed the action steps, be consistent with your action steps, asking for loving support as you make the adjustments.

    3.8.2 Recommend this activity 3 to your partner; with no strings/expectations attached.

GIVING THANKS

I am grateful to all who helped this project to manifest. Your support, encouragement, guidance, inspiration and insights have all been a positive part of my personal evolutionary process and the production of this book. I have given and continue to give each of you my personal thanks.

I do want to acknowledge four sets of life changers for me:-

1. My Parents, Pauline & Christopher (Robin) Edwards. You are for me living examples of the positive generational impact of nurturing each other and family with love and respect while encouraging space for more expressions of personal excellence.

2. My life partner on this journey of life since the summer of 1979, my wife, Maxine Antonette Edwards (Fletcher). It is a direct result of our journey together that I have been inspired to document the systems within this book to enhance the capacity for all who desire experiencing fulfilling long-term relationships.

3. Literal manifestations of answered prayer, our two daughters, Danielle Antoinette Monique and Robyn Alyssa Jade. Girls, it is my heart felt desire to equip you for life that challenged me to develop systems that are principle based yet simplified enough for anyone to understand to such a level that they can take them, live them, evolve with them make them their own and pass them on from generation to generation.

4. My Spiritual Centre – The Universal Centre of Truth for Better Living (of Jamaica). It is through your bible based teachings that I have become more appreciative of the personal reality and truth of Genesis 1: 26-27

A FEW OF THE BOOKS I HAVE READ

An avid reader is not one of the qualities that would be associated with me. However, lifetime learning is a practice I exemplify. Below are a few of the books/authors who have been personally influential for me.

- ✓ Holy Bible – King James Version (KJV) and New International Version (NIV)
- ✓ Any material by T. D. Jakes – e.g. The Great Investment; Loose that Man & Let Him Go; He-Motions
- ✓ The New Thought Christian – William Warch
- ✓ Your Best Life Now – Joel Osteen
- ✓ Spiritual Economics – Eric Butterworth
- ✓ The Energy of Money – Maria Nemeth Ph.D.
- ✓ Don't Worry, Make Money – Richard Carlson Ph.D.
- ✓ Rich Dad Poor Dad – Robert Kiyosaki
- ✓ Richest Man in Babylon – George S. Clason
- ✓ The Success Book – John Randolph Price
- ✓ Who Moved My Cheese – Dr. Spencer Johnson
- ✓ Free & Laughing – Marguerite Orane
- ✓ Night of the Indigo – Michael Holgate
- ✓ Personal Mastery – Courtney Lodge

SPACE FOR STARTING YOUR PERSONAL JOURNAL

www.ingramcontent.com/pod-product-compliance
Lightning Source LLC
Chambersburg PA
CBHW041529090426
42738CB00035B/14